Takin' It to the Streets—

Again

2005-2006 NMI
MISSION EDUCATION RESOURCES

❋ ❋ ❋

MISSIONS BOOKS

THE HEART AND LIFE OF HELEN TEMPLE
A Way with Words
by Debbie Salter Goodwin

IN FAITH ON WINGS
Nazarene Mission Aviation
by Timothy R. Eby

THE MASTER'S BUILDER
The Jerome Richardson Story
by Richard Gammill

ROCKETS, REBELS, AND RESCUES
Living the Life of a Missionary Kid
by Mark and Jeanette Littleton

TAKIN' IT TO THE STREETS—AGAIN
Kansas City Rescue Mission
by Joe Colaizzi

UNTIL WE ALL HAVE NAMES
Stories of Medical Missions
by Bill McCoy

❋ ❋ ❋

ADULT MISSION EDUCATION RESOURCE BOOK

MISSIONS NOT SO USUAL
Edited by Wes Eby

Takin' It to the Streets—

Kansas City Rescue Mission

Joe Colaizzi

Nazarene Publishing House
Kansas City, Missouri

Contents

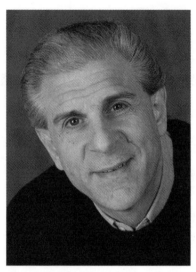

Joe Colaizzi, an ordained elder in the Church of the Nazarene, serves as the director of the Kansas City Rescue Mission. Joe and his family reside in the Kansas City area.

Acknowledgments

I'm indebted to . . .
- the Lord Jesus Christ,
- my supportive, loving family,
- a dedicated, Christ-centered staff,
- a wise board of directors,
- hundreds of volunteers and supporters,
- each person named in these pages without whom there would be no story.

Special thanks to . . .
- Wes Eby for patience, friendship, and expert editing help,
- Gloria Willingham for research and enthusiastic encouragement that prompted me to write, and
- David and Marcia Hayse and Lee and Joan McCleery for a quiet place to do so.

Prologue

When Jesus lifted me
from a dark and hopeless place,
and brought me into the light,
I could never have imagined what He
had in store.
He opened my eyes,
changed my heart, and
grew my faith.
He redirected my career
and led me to a mission field—
the New York City streets.
He introduced me to the Church of the Nazarene,
trained me for ministry,
provided a wife and eventually a family.
The story continues;
it's not yet complete.

"Being confident of this, that he
who began a good work in you will carry it on
to completion until the day of Christ Jesus"
(Philippians 1:6).

Huntersfield Mountain

The paths leading to the top of Huntersfield Mountain had become all too familiar. I'd been climbing them for nearly a week now, up to the top in the morning, and back down to the cottage at night. Searching. Looking for the answer—God's confirmation on the decision I had already made. This search seemed like such a waste.

Dusk was fast approaching on that Friday in late October. After spending all day at the top, I was making my way back down, hoping for a dinner invitation from Roger or his wife, Yvonne. I'd eaten nothing since early Monday morning—breakfast at 30,000 feet as I flew from Kansas City to Albany, New York. Roger met me at the airport, and as we made the 50-mile drive to his home high in the Catskill Mountains, I explained the reason for my surprise visit. I had recently received explicit instructions: *It is hard to hear the Lord's voice in the midst of our busy lives. Find a quiet place to listen, a mountaintop, and seek Him there for direction.*

I'd ignored it the first time. In fact, I pushed it aside each of the four consecutive days I'd heard it in the chapel services at Nazarene Theological Seminary. *This is ridiculous*, I thought. *It can't be from*

God. I mean, let's be realistic. I'm in the middle of my third semester at seminary, seriously struggling to keep up. Assignments will soon be due. I have a job, a working wife, and a 13-month-old son, not to mention we're close to broke. And the only mountaintop I think of every time the preacher suggests it is Huntersfield—1,000 miles and a $600 flight away!

I didn't need a mountaintop . . . or a confirmation. What I needed was to follow through on my decision: leave seminary, gather up my little family, and return to ministry at The Lamb's in New York, or perhaps head west to Los Angeles.

▢ ▢ ▢ ▢

It had been almost two years since Marilyn and I were married. Following a three-week honeymoon in Puerto Rico, we had spent a month on Huntersfield Mountain with Roger and Yvonne Shafer who oversee the activities at Huntersfield Christian Training Center, a place I'd visited whenever I could get away during my single years in New York City. Nestled among the trees halfway up the mountain, hundreds of miles from the deafening noise and lightning fast pace of the city, the center's 580 acres allowed me to retreat into the restful, quiet peace of another world. It was at Huntersfield where the Lord would restore my spirit, nurture my faith, and prepare me for what was to come. I'd become a fast friend with the center's founder and executive director, Rev. Shafer and his wife who, over the years through their strong faith and hard work, had engineered the transformation of what was once a wilderness into a beautifully landscaped sanctuary for learning, rest, recreation, and worship.

Huntersfield was the perfect place to make the transition from Puerto Rico back to New York where a job as building manager, my first paid position in nearly 10 years, was waiting for me at The Lamb's Manhattan Church of the Nazarene. (Until that point in my Christian life, the Lord had directed me to accept no money for work but to simply trust Him.)

The church provided a two-bedroom apartment for us on the recently renovated fifth floor, and in mid-January I began my new adventure as a paid employee. But no sooner had I begun working, I began to sense a prompting to move in a different direction: education and ordination. Seminary was the call. No way! I would not go! And that was final!

I'd been down this road before—at least part way. A year or so before the wedding, while serving at The Lamb's as director of Crisis Care, an outreach to New York City's homeless population, I enrolled in a home-study course offered by the church. My grades were OK, but without peer support and the dynamics of the classroom environment I found study difficult. Then there were the demands and, frankly, the excitement and stimulation of daily ministry constantly luring me away from the books. To graduate would have taken forever. And more to the point, I simply was *not* interested in seminary.

"God has already ordained me," I declared to my good friend Gwen McGuire, the Lamb's chef. "I don't need to be ordained by any man."

"Joseph," she answered, "you have a lot to learn and something to say, and in this man's world it's important to have that paper so people will listen to you."

I didn't want to hear it, but I couldn't shake it. Time and again and from various sources the message became progressively clearer. Slowly, my resistance broke down. Surely this was the Lord's prompting. Reluctantly I finally gave in. With Marilyn's help, I submitted applications to several schools. Our search eventually led to Nazarene Theological Seminary in Kansas City. By late June I'd been accepted and was scheduled to begin classes in September.

By mid-July after only six months as building manager at The Lamb's, we were off to Kansas City. We'd picked up a well-used VW van, stuffed it full with our few possessions, said good-bye to New York, and headed west. Marilyn, now seven months pregnant, would work full-time to support us. I would work part-time and attend seminary.

□ □ □ □

Rusty? An understatement! In over my head? Absolutely! But I'd been called, and I was resolute.

□ □ □ □

With relocation assistance from the seminary and encouragement from just about everyone we met, it wasn't hard to settle in. The Lord led us to a quaint, little one-bedroom house surrounded by a huge, fenced-in front yard not far from school. The racially mixed inner-city neighborhood welcomed us warmly. Finding a church was no problem either. Everyone we met, it seemed, attended Kansas City First Church. Marilyn soon started work at the Church of the Nazarene's International Headquarters, and I found a part-time job as custodian at an Episcopal church. Summer went quickly. School began before I knew it.

Academics had always been a challenge for me. This time was no different. Besides, it had been 17 years since college when I'd studied radio and television communications and earned a bachelor's degree in fine arts, a far cry from theology. Rusty? An understatement! In over my head? Absolutely! But I'd been called, and I was resolute.

As I struggled with theological terminology and waded through tons of reading, attempting to understand mind-stretching concepts that challenged my faith, not to mention the first semester of Greek, our son, Joey, was born. What a joy! With him came another form of education, one of midnight feedings, soiled diapers, and the study of feet and flowers and bugs. He immediately became my best buddy and a very welcome, very *necessary* diversion.

The first two semesters and a course or two of summer school had pushed me to my limit. By the middle of the fall semester that second year, I'd had just about enough. *Lord, I need Your help. This is impossible!*

Comfort and peace came at church and at home; direction was added at seminary chapel services. Those were important. Necessary, in fact. I attended them all.

At the height of my frustration that semester, the chapel speaker cautioned, "It's hard to hear the Lord's voice in the midst of our busy lives." Four times that week he challenged us to "find a quiet place to listen, a mountaintop, and seek Him there for direction."

As he spoke, images of Huntersfield invaded my mind. I resisted. *Ridiculous!* I thought. *That's 1,000 miles from here. It would cost too much time and money! What about Marilyn? The baby? School? My job?* I dismissed the thought.

But the Lord had other ways to reach me.

The Sunday-evening message at First Church brought a similar challenge and stirred the same images of Huntersfield. I could no longer deny it; the Lord was speaking to me again. Driving home that night, I shared my thoughts with Marilyn. Her response came without hesitation, settling the matter quickly.

"If the Lord is speaking to you," she said, "you need to listen. I think you should go. Joey and I will be fine."

Early the next morning I was on a jet heading for Albany. I'd call Roger from the airport.

☐ ☐ ☐ ☐

As we drove back to Huntersfield, I filled Roger in on the details. As always, he seemed to understand completely and committed to pray with me for the direction I needed. Both Roger and Yvonne wel-

View from Huntersfield Mountain

comed me warmly. They set me up across the road from the parsonage in a cottage overlooking the pond. It promised to be the "quiet place to listen" the preacher had challenged us to find.

For the next several days I sought Him; at the cottage, by the pond, in the forest, and up the winding paths all the way to the top of Huntersfield Mountain. I *knew* what He'd say: *School is not for you. You've tried. Now, sell your books, pack your bags, and take your family back to New York.*

Every day I wandered all over that mountain, hiking through the pine forest, across the fire breaks, onto this trail or that one, often making my own, from dawn until dark, climbing, praying, listening, reading, fasting, pleading for the confirmation I expected—even longed for.

By the morning of day five, I was beginning to second-guess myself. I hadn't yet heard anything from the Lord and this whole idea was beginning to seem more like a foolish mistake than a God directed quest for guidance. I just needed to use common sense and do what I knew I should: pack it all up and move on.

At the same time, I was certain He had called me to this mountain. So up I climbed again, continuing to pray, stopping just to listen. Only silence screamed back, driving me higher, closer to the top, closer to the answer, I hoped. Throughout the day I struggled. Still, only silence.

Late that afternoon, knowing dusk would come quickly, I started back down toward the cottage. I decided to head for the parsonage, hoping for dinner. My thoughts raced as I walked. *Why haven't you spoken, Lord? How long do I wait? Was this Your idea or mine?*

About 100 yards from my destination, I stopped. As I stood there alone on the dirt mountain road, consumed by the quiet, dusk began to settle in and tears began to fall.

Lord, please speak to me. What should I do? All I want is Your will. Please reveal it to me. Isn't this why I came? Didn't You call me here?

Uncontrollably I wept. And waited. And then, *Climb back up that mountain and read My Word.*

Lord, I've been reading Your Word all week! And I just came down from that mountain!

Again the thought: *Climb back up that mountain and read My Word.*

Thirty minutes later and several hundred feet higher, I was sitting on a familiar-looking log with my pockekt-sized KJV, focused on Second Timothy chapter two, where I'd left off early that morning.

□ □ □ □

I wished, at that moment,

I could erase those words!

□ □ □ □

Daylight slipped away quickly and with it the ability to see well enough to read. Turning the book in every direction, I strained to read the next verse. I *had* to read it. But that was not to be. Now, galvanized to my heart and imprinted in my mind were the last words I'd read before the lights went out: "Study to shew thyself approved unto God, a workman that needeth not to be ashamed, rightly dividing the word of truth" (2 Timothy 2:15, KJV). I wished, at that moment, I could erase those words! Had I realized I was heading in the direction of that passage I'd have been reading from another book!

But, Lord, I thought, *I mean . . . don't You want me back in New York . . . involved in ministry? I'm not cutting it in school. Don't you see?* But I knew He *did* see; I knew He had spoken. His direction was clear: *Joe, return to Kansas City and complete your studies.*

Slowly and with very mixed emotions, I made my way back down the mountain to the parsonage. Roger and Yvonne smiled when I told them. "We figured that when you first arrived," Roger said. "But we knew you needed to hear it from the Lord," added Yvonne.

Over a late dinner, as our conversation continued, four clear directives emerged: continue with seminary, focus on missions, give up the part-time janitorial job, and get involved with the Kansas City Rescue Mission.

This was not at all what I wanted to hear. Neither did it make any sense. School was impossible, and if I were to continue, we would need my income. Furthermore, even though I'd spent years ministering among the homeless in New York City, my many attempts to get involved with the Rescue Mission during our 15 months in Kansas City had been fruitless. They didn't need my help.

☐ ☐ ☐ ☐

Homecoming was sweet. We'd missed each other. It's amazing how much a one-year-old learns and grows in a week.

As I shared the experiences of my journey with Marilyn, we agreed that whether the directives made sense to me or not they were clearly from the Lord. Why did I need a wilderness experience 1,000 miles away? Why hadn't the Lord spoken to me at home or at least sooner than He had on the mountain? Like the preacher said, "It's hard to hear the Lord's voice in the midst of our busy lives." I needed to completely disengage. I needed the familiar, the quiet of Huntersfield. I needed the encouragement and counsel of Roger and Yvonne. And I needed to come to the place in my heart and mind where I was empty of myself, open to His will, and hungry for it. Only then could I have heard Him.

In faith and with a strange sense of confidence I followed His directives. I rearranged classes, resigned my job, and apprehensively called Rev. Tim Kilby, a local Nazarene pastor who, at that time, was also responsible for the Rescue Mission.

"Tim, I don't understand it, but I believe the Lord is directing me to get involved with the Rescue Mission."

Silence. And then, "That's a miracle!"

"What do you mean?" I asked.

"Did you know that the resident director resigned just this month?"

"Uh . . . no . . . I had no idea."

"And every time I pray about what I should do," Tim continued, "who I should ask to take the position, I see your name and your face in my mind."

"Trust in the LORD with all thine heart; and lean not unto thine own understanding. In all thy ways acknowledge him, and he shall direct thy paths" (Proverbs 3:5-6, KJV).

2
Jarrette Aycock's Legacy

The 49ers were playing the Dolphins that year in Super Bowl XIX. Miami kicked off at 3 P.M. just about the time I officially kicked off my career as executive director of the Kansas City Rescue Mission (KCRM). Marilyn and I were excited. Even if I was the only paid employee, and even when the discussion at my first official District Properties Committee meeting centered on the question, "Should we sell the building and shut down the ministry?" We saw no problems, only opportunities.

A deteriorating turn-of-the-century building had been home for the Mission for more than 22 years. It was a three-story brick structure with a basement, located in the River Market area of Kansas City. Only the basement and first floor were in use and usable.

The ministry, focused primarily toward homeless men, offered hope in Christ through daily chapel services as well as food, shelter, and clothing. A crew of 6 formerly homeless men lived there full-time and handled daily chores—cooking, cleaning, and laundry. They'd take turns answering the only phone in the place. They all assisted with crowd control during the busy times; these occurred daily.

KCRM on Walnut Street, 1962-1991

Every evening 20 or so homeless men converged on the Mission just before the doors closed at 7 P.M. when the 30-minute gospel service began. Then came dinner, a shower, and sleep. Mornings, after breakfast, the overnight guests would leave, and the crew went to work on their chores. A noble plan that, at times, played out somewhat as described but lacked supervision, accountability, and leadership. And that fact energized me. It gave me purpose beyond the books, a tangible outlet to combine and apply New York experience and textbook theory. Through hands-on ministry opportunities to preach, teach, counsel, administrate, dream, and grow, the Mission provided fulfillment. School no longer overwhelmed me. KCRM was a gift.

Homeless people have needs. One is to be needed. I'd learned that firsthand in New York. Kansas City was no different. The Mission building had needs as well. Faucets leaked. Lighting and air circulation were poor. Windows were broken, even missing. Walls needed paint. Doors were broken, and the carpet was worn and torn.

Past experience had taught me the basic skills to address most of these concerns, but I needed help. We had little money for such luxuries. Our total income that first year was less than $32,000. Twenty percent of that had come from the Church of the Nazarene's Kansas City District office, because District Superintendent Milton Parrish was convinced that the Lord wanted the Mission to survive. But I wouldn't ask the district for more money. We needed to find another way.

It was George who first stepped up. That's when he learned he was needed.

The basement shower was dark and dank. Most of the paint had long since peeled from the ancient stone walls. Shower heads leaked profusely, releasing hot water, enough to erode mortar, promote mold, and fill a gallon jug every 60 seconds, wasting 1,440 gallons of hot water every day!

With a couple of rusty old wrenches I'd found among the tools scattered throughout the Mission, I attempted to repair the leak. That's when George offered unsolicited advice, revealing knowledge far beyond mine. I soon learned he'd had a successful career in building maintenance until alcohol got the best of him. He'd been at the Mission off and on for several years. Recently he'd become one of our six crew members. George was a natural leader. Under his direction we quickly repaired the shower. It wasn't long before he became the "foreman" and shaped the rest of the crew into the beginnings of a renovation team. With the tools we gathered and a few minimal supplies, we went to work, room by room. Soon, we were joined by board members and several interested laymen. We repaired the plumbing, installed new chapel lighting, built shelves, carpeted floors, repaired bunks (George even built one), painted walls, improved the ventilation system, and, in general, began to upgrade the looks and function of the entire KCRM facility.

At the same time we worked hard to improve attitudes, meal quality, and the overall safety of the Mission. We improved chapel services and emphasized prayer and reading the Word. All the while we built stronger relationships with our neighbors, the crew, and our homeless friends.

Less popular with some were the new ideas we implemented to enhance ministry standards and services. We raised the behavioral bar for both the resident crew and overnight clients, screening more carefully for drugs, alcohol, and weapons. Clients were no longer granted Mission services while under the influence. Instead they were referred to agencies better equipped to handle them. Threats and violence also became cause for denial of Mission services.

Our objectives were clear. Constantly demonstrate the love of God. Treat clients with respect and dignity. Empower, don't enable them. Encourage them to leave their past behind, seek forgiveness, and reach for a hope-filled future in Christ.

The precedent for those objectives had been set long ago.

□ □ □ □

At eight years old he was chewing tobacco and rolling his own. He was the youngest of eight children, the favorite, pampered by the family. They tried their best to steer him straight, but his knack to find trouble led to fights and mischief most of the time. At age 14 his "bad boy" behavior had exhausted his teacher's patience, forcing him to leave school. With help from his Christian family, he made a fresh start in another state. But there, involvement with the wrong crowd led to drinking whiskey and playing poker. After five failed attempts at five different schools, Jarrette Aycock sold everything he owned, went to the town water tank, and waited for a freight train to anywhere. For years he drifted around the country, hopping freights from city to city. An alcoholic and a wanderer, sometimes a tramp, he gambled and drank. Yet every once in a while, he took on the responsibility of a job.

□ □ □ □

The place was filled with derelicts, drunks, dope addicts, and all the odds and ends of skid row.

□ □ □ □

One night, though holding down a job at the time, a bitter and dejected Aycock walked along skid row in Los Angeles, cigarette hanging from his lips, the fumes of whiskey on his breath. The sound of a gospel song stopped him cold. There between two open saloons he saw the Union Rescue Mission. "Go in lad," a stranger said, "you might hear something that would do you good." As he walked through the doorway, he noticed a sign that read "There is hope for all who enter here."

"The place was filled with derelicts, drunks, dope addicts, and all the odds and ends of Skid Row," Aycock later reported. "As I sat there looking them over, I got to thinking that I had been like them before and that I would be like them again unless I could somehow get free of all the old habits and the ceaseless downward pull that had plagued my life for years."[1]

The speaker that evening was Mel Trotter, himself a hopeless drunk until, on the brink of suicide, he met the Savior at the Pacific Garden Mission in Chicago. Trotter became an evangelist, and for the next 40 years established over 60 rescue missions across the country.

Aycock listened as Mel Trotter shared the story about how Jesus had changed his life. Then others shared their stories.

"Some of them seemed to be telling my story," Aycock wrote. "They told of years of wandering, bound by sin and habits, loss of friends, loved ones, and a disappointed, brokenhearted mother."[2]

An invitation followed the testimonies, and Jar-

Dr. Jarrette Aycock, founder of KCRM

rette Aycock made a difficult but very necessary decision.

"It took a tremendous effort," he wrote, "because before we are ready to ask Jesus to give us a new life, we really have to be sick of the old one. We have to know that the person we have been so pleased with and proud of for so many years, the person we have pampered and almost ruined, isn't really any good at all and won't be any good until we let Jesus Christ rule that life. That isn't an easy decision. But the results of it are all glorious. I know because I made the decision myself that night, and Christ has never failed me."[3]

At the altar of a rescue mission, Jarrette Aycock walked away from his troubled past and into a hope-filled future. After working for a short while at another mission, he then began studying for the ministry. Two years after his conversion Aycock married Dell Davis. He entered the evangelistic field the following year and was ordained five years later in the Church of the Nazarene, where he served for 32 years as an evangelist.

In 1942, now Dr. Jarrette Aycock became superintendent of the Kansas City District. In 1950 he founded the Kansas City Nazarene Rescue Mission that three years later became the Kansas City Rescue Mission. Here the objective would be that others would have the same opportunity young Jarrette Aycock had received years before.

I learned a lot about the Mission during that first year as executive director. It had been anything but smooth sailing from the outset. Originally located at 916 East 12th Street, the Mission had moved four times during its first five years in operation. Then the building at 523 Walnut Street was purchased.[4] It had been the Mission's home for nearly 23 years. Leadership had also changed much, at least 11 times during the Mission's first 35 years.[5]

Dr. Aycock worked hard, even after his retirement, to keep the Mission's door open. As his mantle was passed on, it eventually rested on the shoulders of Milton Parrish who, along with C. W. "Bud" King, then president of the Mission's Board of Directors, and Dean Quillin, board secretary, was equally determined to see the ministry succeed. They became a strong support and encouragement to me.

---

1. Jarrette Aycock, *He Lifted Me* (Kansas City: Beacon Hill Press of Kansas City), 17.
2. Aycock, 18.
3. Aycock, 18-19.
4. See appendix A for a list of locations.
5. See appendix B for a list of the directors of KCRM.

3

Hobo Jungle

Involvement in ministry brought balance to my life. School had become manageable and life at KCRM was stimulating. Joey was growing and a real favorite among the homeless. With Marilyn's help, the bills at home were paid, and the Mission was becoming more organized. We were on a roll.

I learned that the question "Should we sell the building and shut down the ministry?" raised at that first official meeting with the Properties Committee had a lot to do with the city's plans to redevelop the River Market area. The Mission building was in the middle of it. We'd have to move. But I'd also learned from the chairperson of the Market Area Redevelopment Committee that we could stay for at least another year and a half. In fact the city's official redevelopment plan stated that it could be as long as seven years before we'd need to leave. *Plenty of time*, I thought. *Let's nurture the ministry, work on this building, and see what God does.*

Diligently we continued making improvements. One of the neediest areas was the kitchen. Lighting was poor. Equipment was old and deteriorating. Paint was faded and worn. But the greatest concern was filth, and the Health Department refused to renew our Food Service Permit. Talk about an opportunity. So the guys went to work. They replaced bare lightbulbs with donated used fluorescent fixtures, scrubbed down the equipment, and painted the ceiling, walls, and floor. Then I called the Health Department. Quietly, breathlessly, I stood in the background as the inspector carefully examined the entire room. Forty-five minutes seemed like an eternity. Then looking down at the ancient but very clean stove he said with conviction, "Well, there must be a God, 'cause He sure did a miracle in this place!"

□ □ □ □

But his attitude remained unchanged. Sam was an angry man.

□ □ □ □

Sam was another miracle. It was bitter cold that February night when we met. He was trying to sell me his radio for cigarettes and beer money. He'd been staying in an unheated room above a bar several doors from the Mission. He was a stocky little fellow with a bad attitude, considered the "town drunk" by most. I invited him to give up his cold room for the warmth of a bed at the Mission. He gladly accepted. Sam came to the altar every night that first week, then asked if I'd take him to church on Sunday. He listened close to the sermon. He seemed to understand, said he wanted to get right with God and prayed with the pastor to accept Jesus. That evening at the Mission Sam testified before all of his drinking buddies, "I don't know what happened," he said, "but the tears was rollin' from my eyes, my knees was shakin', an' my heart flip-flopped a few times. But I know this, Jesus is real!"

Staying sober, however, remained a problem for Sam. We'd talk and pray, but Sam needed more. So after prayer and much discussion we invited Sam to join the crew. To everyone's pleasant surprise, he was a hard worker. But his attitude remained unchanged. Sam was an angry man.

It was midafternoon on Wednesday when a large donation of cleaning and personal hygiene supplies arrived. Sam had finished with his laundry assignment and offered to help take inventory of the new shipment. He did well, even demonstrated fine organizational skills and obviously enjoyed the work. I was called away and told Sam we'd finish tomorrow. He wanted to continue. I approved. At day's end he still had more to do, but for the first time since I'd met him Sam's attitude was upbeat and optimistic. And he wanted to finish the next day. I was thrilled. I'd found the solution to Sam's problem: responsibility and empowerment to use his organizational skills. Throughout the evening Sam's attitude remained positive. Others on the crew recognized it as well.

The next day Sam picked up where he'd left off. Still his attitude was positive. This was a miracle. Sam was a changed man. Late on the third day he finished. My objective now was to keep him busy, organizing *anything*. I assigned him to the clothing room. It wasn't the same. This was not a stimulating task for Sam. We tried the food pantry next, again no interest. Even worse, his sour attitude returned.

Several days later a client who'd helped unload

the donation that Sam had organized asked for some mouthwash. He'd carried several cases upstairs. We searched the entire storage area but found nothing. Not one case. Not one *bottle*. I called for Sam, but he wasn't around. So I asked another crew member if he knew where the mouthwash might be.

"Gone!" he said.

"Gone? How could it be *gone?"* I asked. "Where did it *go?"*

"That mouthwash was 25 percent alcohol," he whispered.

Ouch! I'd invited Sam to a party. Right there in the Mission. He'd drunk three cases of mouthwash in as many days. So much for organizational skills.

I was upset, probably more with myself than with Sam. I wouldn't need to learn *this* lesson again! We had a long talk when he returned. Timidly, he confessed and meekly asked forgiveness. Though he continued to struggle, Sam made steady progress. He attended church regularly and was soon baptized. We helped him enroll in a 16-week Salvation Army rehabilitation program, after which Sam was clean, sober, and regularly reading the Bible in his own apartment.

The incident with Sam and our intolerance for alcohol eventually led to the purchase of an electronic device that would measure respiratory alcohol content.

I was startled when I overheard a chronic alcoholic mission "regular" say to the evening supervisor. "Usin' this machine is the best thing you guys ever did!"

Sam being baptized

Curious, I asked him why.

"I like this place," he said. "It's clean and safe, and I know if I wanna stay here I need to come in sober. Havin' to face this little machine every night forces me to stay sober all day."

Our strategy was working.

While Sam was organizing mouthwash that first day, I'd been called away to meet a man. He introduced himself as Ray. He was looking for work. He and his nine-year-old son Jarred* were staying in a nearby apartment in exchange for custodial work. Ray

---

*Not his real name.

was a painter. He'd been in business with a partner who'd walked off with his share of the assets, forcing the business to close, leaving Ray unemployed. Ray had found several part-time-below-minimum-wage jobs but needed full-time with better pay. We had nothing to offer but friendship, faith, and food. Ray took me up on the friendship and food.

For several months Ray searched unsuccessfully for work while Jarred was in school earning A's. They came nightly to the Mission for dinner. Ray kept his distance spiritually, but he'd listen when I prayed. Meanwhile, our family ministered to Jarred: baseball games, the circus, picnics, Sesame Street on Ice, church, and church camp. Still no job for Ray.

In April they were given 30 days to vacate their apartment. The River Market Redevelopment project was closing in. We moved them into the Mission and began to look for options. I learned of a new HUD program soon to be launched "Operation Homeless." Seventy-five qualified homeless individuals or families in Kansas City would be awarded certificates guaranteeing rent subsidy up to 100 percent, depending on a person's income. Ray was among the first to qualify. A prayer answered. He searched diligently for an apartment but to no avail. "No children allowed." "No two-bedroom apartments available." "Already rented." "Two-year waiting list."

As a last resort I wrote a letter explaining Ray's situation and sent it to the Mission's few supporters. Two days later one of those supporters called. He had a two-bedroom house available. The following Sunday, I learned later, a pastor built a sermon around my letter which he read to his congregation. This prompted a lady in that congregation to call the Mission with a job offer for Ray and some new clothes for Jarred. Ray was hired that same day. More answered prayers. Still, Ray remained resistant to Christianity, but he allowed Jarred to attend church regularly with Marilyn, Joey, and me.

Stories like these revealed the Lord's fingerprints all over the Mission. This in turn stimulated increasing volunteer interest and involvement. Pastors, seminary students, laypeople, groups, and individuals assisted daily with chapel services, meals, special holiday events, and creative new ideas.

In the tradition of the Lamb's we began serving a first-class Thanksgiving Day feast.

At Christmas a special buffet meal and gifts of stocking caps, gloves, razors, and toothbrushes followed the Christmas story and the singing of carols.

Super Bowl Sunday inspired the beginning of a new tradition: hot dogs, chips, and dips served during a large-screen TV presentation of the game and a half-time gospel service.

Churches and Sunday School classes invited the crew and other Mission clients to concerts, dinners, sporting events, dramatic presentations, and fishing trips. Vans were sent on Sunday mornings to transport anyone interested to church. We put together a touch football team and fielded the first ever KCRM softball team. We even played in a church league.

The increased activities and overall improvements to the building and services drew additional clients, eventually nearly 50 a day. This stretched us

KCRM softball team.
Joe Colaizzi, kneeling on right, with Joey

all. We needed help we couldn't afford. So I asked my pastor, Rev. Keith Wright, for prayer support.

That's when Lyn showed up. She'd recently told the pastor she would like to volunteer some of her time to a worthy cause. I didn't hesitate. Neither did Lyn. For the next 18 months, in addition to coordinating some of the volunteer activities, Lyn arranged for medical and nursing home care, prescriptions, optical appointments, and dental care for the crew and our clients. She even figured out a way for Bill, our 64-year-old cook, to acquire a hearing aid—at no cost! Then Legal Aid stepped in and assisted Bill in getting his Social Security disability insurance, enabling him to move into an apartment of his own. No longer dependent on the Mission, Bill was now able to pay his own way and enjoy the dignity of senior citizenship.

□ □ □ □

The Jungle is like another world, an easy place to get lost or to lose your identity.

□ □ □ □

Not even Lyn could get the clothing room organized. It remained a constant problem. Even the volunteers struggled with it. After my experience with Sam, I was a bit leery when Lonny asked if he could build some racks and organize the room. My doubt was based on the fact that before joining the crew Lonny had been living outdoors in a campsite in the "Hobo Jungle," a wooded strip of land populated by drifters and vagrants several blocks from the Mission. Recognizing my skepticism, Lonny outlined a plan, assuring me he was up to the task. With not much to lose I finally agreed, and Lonny went to work. While he labored diligently, we had many conversations about the Lord. Lonny was receptive and eventually opened his heart. He soon finished the project, but after only about six weeks he disappeared. Unsuccessfully, we searched the Mission and the neighborhood. My instincts said he'd probably returned to the Jungle. So off I went to search.

The Jungle is like another world, an easy place to get lost or to lose your identity. Some have lost

A camp site in Hobo Jungle

their lives there. Literally on the edge of downtown, this densely wooded strip stretches along the railroad tracks beside the Missouri River for what seems like miles. The Jungle isn't the safest place to explore, but that sunshiny spring afternoon took the edge off. I plowed through hundreds of yards of brush, sighting several camps along the way but no life. Making my way through a particularly thick section, I noticed a large clearing ahead. Ducking low branches and stepping over and around the underbrush, I carefully made my way to the clearing. It was about 50 feet across. The stones surrounding the space clearly marked it as private. Inside the circle furthest from where I stood was a makeshift shelter. At the edge closest to me was a neatly built stone fire pit about 12 inches high. The man squatting in front of it cooking didn't bother to look up.

"You lost pal?" he asked.

"I'm lookin' for a guy named Lonny," I explained.

"Don't know no Lonny."

Just then the door to the shelter opened. A familiar smiling face peered out at me. Lonny had recognized my voice. He was happy to see me and invited me inside. The shelter was about 12 feet square and 7 feet high. It was made up of wood scraps, logs, and bits and pieces of this and that. It was covered with discarded sheets of plastic, trash bags and other water resistant materials. Empty wooden crates served as chairs, a beat-up old couch lined the back wall. As we visited, Lonny's friend who didn't "know no Lonny" stepped in and offered coffee. I accepted.

Lonny thanked me for looking him up and for introducing him to Jesus. "But," he said, "I need my freedom." He wasn't interested in returning to the Mission.

I encouraged him to come back, but I understood. As we talked it eventually dawned on me: where do two homeless, unemployed men living in the Jungle get coffee? So I asked.

"Oh," Lonny said beaming, "we go up to the corner restaurant in the market every morning and get fresh grounds from their Dumpster."

Somehow the coffee quickly lost its appeal. Overall it had been a good visit: Lonny was OK, he'd assured me his faith was intact, and I'd survived the coffee and my first visit to the Jungle.

4

Tangled Limbs
and Displaced
Pews

As the ministry developed so did the Mission's Board of Directors. During our second year with the Mission, Carl Lee Aubrey agreed to serve as treasurer. Along with financial expertise and strong leadership skills, Carl brought a deep love for the Lord, the Mission, and the lost, and a sincere personal friendship, all immeasurably beneficial to the Mission and to me.

Building on the efforts of those who'd gone before, we were strengthening the foundation on which the Mission would build its future. I was convinced the Mission had a future. The indications were strong: changed lives, volunteer interest and involvement, and increased support. And although the River Market Redevelopment was picking up steam, the developer had assured me of a second 18-month extension before we'd have to move.

During those first 2 years we helped 7 men find full-time jobs and 19 homeless people find housing. And 14 that we know of, including Sam and Lonny, made a serious commitment to Jesus Christ. And then there's Jarred. He attended church with our family almost every Sunday for a year after he and his dad, Ray, moved into their house. One morning he surprised us with the news—he'd given his heart to Jesus "awhile back."

It took four years for me to complete seminary, two and a half of them included the Mission. As a result, two events occurred almost simultaneously: seminary graduation and ordination as an elder in the Church of the Nazarene. When we left New York, Marilyn and I both assumed we'd return after graduation. The Lord had other plans. He had more for us to do at the Mission. We welcomed the challenge.

It wasn't long before a call came from Steve Kmetz, another recent seminary graduate. Steve was interested in inner-city ministry, and offered to volunteer his time as he learned. Poor health had taken Lyn off the volunteer rolls, leaving a void that Steve was delighted to fill.

Steve was a perfect fit. He had the heart of a servant and a deep commitment to Christ and the poor. His personality and skills were exactly what we needed. Steve handled what I couldn't. No task was beneath him, none too difficult. He nurtured the crew spiritually, helping to lay the foundation for KCRM's Christian Development Program for recovery. He worked along with the crew and volunteers to further improve and maintain the building. He handled scheduling, special projects, and recreational activities. Steve's creative input, enthusiastic personality, and high energy inspired us all. With Steve's help we knew we could develop an even more effec-

**Joe Colaizzi at seminary graduation
with Marilyn and Joey**

tive ministry. So with Mission finances slowly but
steadily increasing, we hired him.

Together with the board, we dreamed exciting
dreams of counseling, case management, education,
job training, housing, and follow-up for every client.
But our dreams reached far beyond our limited resources. About that same time we learned of a new
direct-mail fund-raising program, specifically designed to assist small missions, such as ours. After
much prayer and discussion we decided to sign on.

Results came quickly. So did the criticism. The
program was inflexible and tended to misrepresent
the Mission. This triggered some nasty reports in the
Kansas City Star newspaper that, in turn, created
havoc for the Mission staff, the board, and the dis-

trict superintendent. Unable to correct the problems, we dissolved our contract after less than two months. In that short period, however, the program had attracted a significant number of new donors, more than doubling our support base. We were now one small step closer to the fulfillment of our dreams—the hard way.

The brightest moment in the midst of all the confusion and stress, occurred when Marilyn gave birth to our second child, a spunky little sweetheart of a girl we named Janna. Instantly, she became Joey's best friend and a joy to the whole family. She was a breath of fresh air with an enthusiasm for life that was contagious and a blessing to us all.

Meanwhile, as the demands of ministry continued to increase, the Lord sent another volunteer, Betty Rutledge, a recently retired legal secretary, who wanted to make a difference for the Lord. She did. It was Betty who handled the phones, maintained the files, organized the office, and did the typing, the banking, and the encouraging. Overall, Betty helped establish a more functional, efficient operation. Along with Betty came another blessing— Clarence, her husband, a retired truck driver who volunteered to serve as the Mission's courier.

I was grateful for the help. The load was increasing. Chapel services were planned 365 days a year. I had inherited a roster of about 30 speakers, each scheduled to speak one night a month. But when someone didn't show, which unfortunately happened quite often, I had an opportunity to fill in. Some days were routine, others had an interesting twist.

**Joe Colaizzi with Joey and Janna
visiting with KCRM guests**

□ □ □ □

The noise in the back of the chapel was growing louder, distracting both the congregation and me as I preached. As a rule we closed the Mission doors shortly after chapel began to encourage folks who knew the routine to show up on time. But it wasn't worth a fight. I signaled the crew to open the doors. Bursting into the room, eyes fixed on mine, a stranger walked quickly down the center isle straight toward me. I was standing directly in front of the knee-high altar rail. Two more steps and he'd knock me backward over the altar. When I raised my hands to signal stop he lunged, wrestling me to the floor. Shocked and in disbelief, my instincts took control. Leverage was everything. I moved quickly, waiting for certain and sudden assistance from my loyal congregation. "Uh!" I jockeyed for position. Twisting, rolling, squirming, we ended up under the second or third pew. I was on the bottom but somehow had the advantage. I'd worked my way behind him, slipped my arms under his, and locked my fingers together behind his neck. My legs, crossed at the ankles, were locked around his waist. It was over as quickly as it had started.

"If you promise to settle down brother," I said, panting for breath, "I'll let you go."

"OK, I promise," he panted back.

□ □ □ □

The six-inch steel blade of his hunting knife flashed in my face.

□ □ □ □

Untangling our limbs we made our way from under the displaced pews. Both of us still gasping for breath, we stood to our feet, eyes locked on each other, as we straightened our clothes.

"If I wanted to hurt you, man," he said as he reached behind his back, "I would've used this!" The six-inch steel blade of his hunting knife flashed in my face. "I just wanted to talk to the preacher," he said.

He helped me straighten the pews, and I offered him a seat. Then I glanced around the room. There sat my faithful congregation, casually observing the action. No one had lifted a finger. (Maybe they'd been praying, or thought this was an illustration!)

As it turned out the stranger simply wanted to speak with someone in charge to register his complaint that the Mission doors were closed during chapel and dinner. He'd interpreted my signal to stop as an aggressive move and responded accordingly. Some days were like that. This was the first and last time anything like that happened at the Mission. More than anything it served as a wake-up call to set procedures in place that would stop these kinds of things from happening in the future.

I enjoyed preaching, but it consistently demanded much of my time. That is, until Bill Hunt showed up. He'd been a bivocational pastor with the Church of God Holiness and was soon to retire from Hallmark Cards. A recent addition to the preaching schedule, Bill was often accompanied by his wife, Elaine, who assisted on the piano. They soon earned the status of favorites among our homeless guests. At Bill's invitation, we met over breakfast to discuss an idea he thought might interest me.

"Why not teach a Bible study every evening prior to the service?" he suggested. "That way the men can come inside earlier, get out of the cold, and hear the Word. If they don't want to listen, fine, but at least they'll be inside where it's warm, and chances are they'll hear something that'll help them."

I was skeptical. "And who would teach this Bible study, Bill?"

"I will," he quickly responded.

"You're talking seven nights a week?"

"Yes. Elaine and I will come down as soon as I finish work."

"Seven nights a week is a serious commitment, Bill."

Elaine and Bill Hunt, long-time volunteers at KCRM

"Joe Colaizzi, I believe this is from the Lord. I've always wanted to teach, and I would like to volunteer my time to do it."

This seemed like one of those too-good-to-be-true situations. We agreed to pray about it. In the meantime, Bill would lay out a year's worth of Bible study outlines. I'd check his references.

Top people at both Hallmark Cards and the Church of God Holiness couldn't say enough good about Bill. And so it was for the next 11 years. The Lord provided a musician to play and a chaplain to preach, when necessary, and teach—seven nights a week 365 days a year.

The timing couldn't have been more perfect. By

this time daily chapel attendance had increased to an average of 48 a day. Then there were the half-dozen or so stragglers, the neighborhood mavericks. I'd met them early on. We had their attention also. But they seldom stayed or even ate at the Mission. They preferred the outdoors, the Jungle, or the third floor of the abandoned bank building several doors from the Mission. Like Lonny, they wanted their freedom. They respected what we did but were constantly pushing the limits: challenging the staff, our standards, and our clients, not to mention the neighbors. Tim was one of the mavericks.

He couldn't remember much when he arrived. Drug and alcohol addiction had led him into the wrong part of town where he suffered a severe beating, leaving him barely alive and unable to walk. He had temporary amnesia and was incapable of speaking in more than one-word sentences. Several months of rehab helped enable him to walk, but the frustration of chronic memory problems and the realization that he'd "failed at life" led to an unsuccessful suicide attempt and a five-year stretch of living in abandoned buildings and eventually a campsite in the Jungle.

Scrounging around for food, clothing, and occasional shelter, drunkenness, fighting, and jail became a way of life. Trapped in the streets by the memories he *could* recall, vivid reminders of the family he'd pushed away and the job he'd lost, coupled with the short-term memory loss, Tim was convinced he'd never be functional again. "I could not find forgiveness or forgive myself," he told us later. "The only way to hold the guilt back was to drink, and the best place to drink was the River Market area. The Mission was there. The Salvation Army would come down nightly to feed us from the soup wagon, and the police usually wouldn't bother me."

We had our work cut out for us with Tim. We weren't at all certain where to begin, so we simply listened, we cared, and we loved him. Slowly, the healing process, which would ultimately take years, began—physical, emotional, and spiritual alike. Eventually Tim became well enough to discuss, even debate with us, the existence of God and to seek work at the nearby labor pool. He even tried our budding Christian Development Program (CDP) for recovery for a few weeks, but his drinking remained a problem. Nevertheless, we wouldn't quit. We were in this for the long haul.

While our primary focus was on people like Tim and other homeless clients, the Lord was attracting attention in other ways. Kevin, a substance-abuse counselor, had been working with the men on the crew, all now participants in the CDP. Following an afternoon group counseling session, Kevin called me aside and asked if I'd write down the scripture references that had been especially meaningful to me when I accepted Christ. I suggested that we search them out together. As we looked into the Word, I told him how Jesus had changed my life. "Joe," Kevin said, "you have what I want, and I'm willing to do what you did to get it!" He'd come to offer some wonderful counsel, and he left with the Wonderful Counselor in his heart.

5

No Legal Legs

Redevelopment of the River Market was well under way by now. According to the city's official plan it could still be as long as three and a half years before we'd have to move. That plan, however, also made provision for the developer to accelerate the redevelopment process if necessary. This had been attempted several times over the years, each time unsuccessfully, each time pushing the Mission's deadline to move closer to the originally projected date. In any case, the developer was required to "identify needs of Displaced Occupants and Displaced Businesses with special consideration given to [the] . . . nature of business, [and the] availability of suitable replacement facilities."* We were not worried. We were protected. The plan promised assistance. Our experience suggested we had time. Besides, we were busy pursuing our dreams and seeking ways to finance them.

It was May when the tremors began. Plans to accelerate the redevelopment process were in place once again. Acquisition of our property was now scheduled for early July, 25 months away, cutting

---

*Old Town Redevelopment Corporation Amended Plan, page 15.

our time to relocate by more than one third. While we hoped for another reprieve, we cautiously put our dreams on hold and began to search for a new location.

Ten months later our deadline, July 1, was confirmed. We had 15 months to move. This time there would be no extension. The pressure was mounting.

Questions, doubts, and fears crowded in. We had not yet found a new location; we had no money, no clear direction, and very little time. How could we survive? Even if we did, where would we go? Showing up in a new neighborhood with 50 homeless men could present some problems. I'd heard stories of missions in other cities pushed out. We needed a miracle!

A small glimmer of hope flickered the same day our deadline was confirmed. I received a call from the Kansas City chapter of the American Institute of Architects (AIA). Completely unaware of our situation, they asked if KCRM might have a project that would interest their Committee on Housing for the Homeless. We did.

With the committee's help we established selection criteria and accelerated our search for a new location.

The tsunami hit in April. Redevelopment plans were moving even faster than earlier anticipated. Our deadline had moved to November 1, slashing our time to move from 14 months to 6! Just before the holidays and on the threshold of winter, this was a crucial time for the homeless. I requested more time. None was granted. The pressure increased.

Frankly, I was desperate.
Outwardly, I tried to remain calm.
Inwardly, I was a wreck.

By this time the Mission's Board of Directors, now under the leadership of recently elected president Carl Lee Aubrey, had agreed that unless the Lord closed the door we would do whatever was necessary to relocate. A committee of KCRM board members was established to strategize negotiations with the developer. I met at least weekly with that committee. But, try what we would, our attempts to negotiate for more time proved unsuccessful. This became painfully clear the day the sheriff stopped by to serve condemnation papers against the Mission. We needed help!

We'd contacted a half-dozen lawyers to that point in search of legal assistance but to no avail. In fact, the best of the bunch had told me, "You guys don't have a legal leg to stand on." Frankly, I was desperate. Outwardly, I tried to remain calm. Inwardly, I was a wreck.

As a last ditch effort, I sent a letter of appeal to the mayor of Kansas City. I'd received no response. We were striking out, and our precious time was rapidly dwindling, along with my confidence. *Lord*, I prayed, *just help us get through the winter.*

The pressure lifted momentarily when the developer told me, "We're not committed to November first. We'll remain flexible." But the letter he sent a month later stated, "It is our intention to proceed with rehabilitation of your building on an immediate basis." My emotions were all over the board. I was at the end of myself. We'd tried everything. Nothing had worked. We were losing our fight for survival.

A week later I received another letter, this one from the developer's attorney. They were offering $75,000 for our building. It seemed like a fair offer. But they gave us only days to respond, and we needed more time. I let him know this.

Meanwhile, I was asked to share our situation with the Wednesday night prayer group at church. After hearing the story, the church began to pray. "This is Your Mission, Lord. Close it if You will. We do not want to stand in Your way. But if You want the ministry to continue, please make a way." That's when I released it.

Days later I received word that we'd been granted more time to consider the offer to purchase our building. We had 18 additional days to respond. The catch was that the condemnation action against the Mission would also begin in 18 days! We were put on formal notice to vacate our property by October 25, only 90 days away!

As the clock wound down, the AIA Committee took the lead. Together we examined 18 properties and researched 10 others. So far, none would work. Discouraged but not yet defeated, we stubbornly held on to a sliver of hope.

The city's plan required the developer to offer displaced River Market residents several alternative locations. We were offered five. One was too small. Another, was condemned, already scheduled for demolition. The third was not even for sale, and the fourth required extensive repair, "a total gut and rehab" according to the salesman. The owner of the fifth one refused to show us the building.

Emotions came in rapid succession: disappointment, hope, humiliation, anger, hope renewed, frustration. But we would not quit until the Lord made it clear.

Our search for a new location continued.

6

David and Goliath?

About two weeks after the prayer meeting, I received a call from David Goldstein, a reporter with the *Kansas City Star.* He had no idea what had been happening; he simply wanted to know if the redevelopment plans would affect the Mission in any way.

"Yes," I said.

"Would you be willing to discuss it?"

"Yes," again.

The following morning David stopped by and we talked.

"What did he say?" David asked when he learned I had written to the mayor several weeks earlier.

"He hasn't responded yet," I replied.

"Would you mind if I call him?"

I didn't.

Two days later the mayor called me. He wanted to schedule a meeting to discuss the matter in an attempt to find an equitable agreement between the developer and the Mission. This fact was reported in David's article.

The mayor appointed the assistant city manager to conduct the meeting. The developer came alone. I brought my associate, Steve, and the chairman of the AIA Committee.

"Let me get this straight," the assistant city manager said as the meeting came to a close. "I'm not only dealing with the Mission but with the entire Church of the Nazarene *and* with God?"

I thought he summed it up quite nicely.

As our search for a new location dragged on so did our pursuit of a lawyer. When I spoke with my friend Steve Burger, executive director of the International Union of Gospel Missions,* he connected me with a lawyer friend who told me of several real estate lawyers who might be able to help.

More out of a sense of duty than with any hopes or expectations, I started with the first name on my list and began calling. Somehow I got right through. Hurriedly, I explained our situation to Sherwin Epstein. I was certain he, too, would be unable to assist us. I finished my story and waited for the anticipated response.

"I can help you," I thought I heard him say.

"Pardon me?" I said in disbelief.

"I can help you," he repeated. "I've been on different sides of issues with this developer before. I can help you."

Could it be? After months of struggle, worry, and frustration, was a door beginning to open?

---

*The International Union of Gospel Missions, now the Association of Gospel Rescue Missions, headquartered in Kansas City, Missouri, is an association of more than 300 rescue missions worldwide.

He suggested we meet the following morning and asked that I bring along any related paper work.

Loaded down with documentation I arrived a few minutes early for our meeting. On the table beside me I noticed several photocopies of a *Corporate Report** magazine article that featured a familiar name—Sherwin Epstein.

The article reported that Mr. Epstein had recently been selected by his peers as the "best in his field of real estate" and had been listed in the second edition of *The Best Lawyers in America*. And here I sat waiting for an appointment.

Following introductions and pleasantries, Sherwin flipped through the paperwork as we discussed what seemed to me an impossible situation.

His response surprised me. "Remember how the Lord honored Abraham's faith? And how He parted the Red Sea for Moses? Remember how He sent His angel to rescue Peter from prison?"

"You sound like a Christian!" I said in a half-serious tone.

"I *am* a Christian," he said smiling. "So are my wife and children."

Then, in short order, Sherwin determined that he had enough to work with and agreed to represent us. I was beginning to feel like David about to go after the giant.

When David Goldstein's article appeared in the *Star*, several TV reports and a few sympathetic newspaper articles followed.

---

*Corporate Report, February 1987, 35.

The word was out—Kansas City Rescue Mission needed help. And the community began to respond: Realtors, architects, engineers, contractors, unions, and individuals, all offered assistance. None were asking for pay. I was ecstatic! We were still in a fix, but it was clear, the Lord was in control. Why had it taken so long to release this problem to Him?

As the building search narrowed to two possible options, the AIA Committee helped us formulate a plan. With input from our board, staff, residents, and clients, they developed a lengthy document proposing a functional layout for the future Mission facility.

The committee also brought the University of Kansas School of Architecture and Urban Design on board. Fifteen teams of two fifth-year architectural students would be assigned a class project: creating design solutions for the new Kansas City Rescue Mission.

A week after my first meeting with Sherwin, my pastor, Keith Wright, was elected superintendent of the Kansas City District. At 9 A.M. the morning after his election, Carl Lee Aubrey and I visited Pastor Wright's office, his first official meeting as district superintendent.

The Mission's situation would require a continuation of the same staunch district support we'd been receiving from the retiring superintendent, Dr. Milton Parrish. We needed to know.

Our question was quickly answered. There was no doubt. Keith Wright was clearly on board.

As we evaluated each of the two buildings under consideration, the university student design teams were assigned. Eight teams would tackle one build-ing, seven the other. Our need for a licensed architect to tie the student's ideas together was met through Norb Smith, who volunteered to take the job.

By this time we had located a fund-raiser with the necessary skills and expertise to raise the $390,000 we thought we'd need to purchase and renovate either of the two buildings. Requests for funds were sent to foundations throughout the Kansas City area. Among them was an appeal to Hallmark Cards requesting a grant of $30,000 over a two-year period.

In late September about a month before we were required to move, Sherwin called to say the condemnation hearing had been cancelled. Also, he'd set up a conference call meeting with the developer, and wanted me to attend. I was overjoyed!

The day after the hearing was to have taken place, Sherwin and I sat in his office with a speaker phone between us; the developer and his lawyer were on the other end of the line.

"Sure, Sherwin, we can do that. What else would you like?" said the developer's lawyer. "What would work out best for the Mission?"

I was stunned.

They didn't seem to be able to do enough to ac-commodate us, quite a distance from where we started months earlier.

As it turned out, Sherwin's efforts netted us $80,000 for our River Market facility and another $10,500 for moving expenses.

Also, the redevelopment plan required a $500

cash allotment to any River Market resident displaced by the project. Since the participants in our Christian Development Program were residing at the Mission, each of them received $500.

Furthermore, our move date was extended from October 25 to April 1—past the cold winter months and into spring, exactly what we prayed for.

7

Reinforcements

While Sherwin was negotiating with the developer, the board had made its final decision on which new property to pursue. They settled on a 14,000 square foot, single-story, warehouse complex, consisting of two buildings and a parking lot, located at 1520 Cherry Street in downtown Kansas City, Missouri. Asking price—$250,000.

When the settlement for the River Market property was final, negotiations to purchase the Cherry Street property began.

The new KCRM property on Cherry Street

Our fund-raising goal remained $390,000. That is, until we received a professional contractors estimate of $559,200. And that was for renovation only. It did not include the purchase price, moving expenses, furnishings, or legal fees. These would raise the total cost to nearly $1 million, another seemingly impossible goal.

Discouraged again but still not defeated, we proceeded in faith. Money hadn't stopped us before. Besides, this was obviously the Lord's project. We knew He had the resources.

Our list of grants requested would soon total $350,000. Added to the $90,000 we'd just received from the city, we were well on our way.

And we couldn't overlook the many offers of donated building materials, supplies, and volunteer assistance that we continued to receive. These would decrease renovation expenses considerably.

Incorporating design ideas suggested by the KU students, architect Norb Smith fine-tuned the construction drawings, while other volunteers prepared mechanical and electrical plans. Retired contractor Glenn Ford volunteered to manage the project. Board member and builder Roy Campbell agreed to assist him.

In January, negotiations for the Cherry Street property finally settled at $215,000—14 percent below the asking price. The seller then asked if we could use the adjacent two buildings to the north. "We can use them," I replied, "but we can't afford them."

"If you can use them," he said, "you can *have* them."

Glenn Ford, project manager

The two donated buildings alone were equal in square footage to the building we had just sold for $80,000. Our new location now consisted of four buildings totaling 24,000 square feet of usable space, two-and-a-half times more than our old facility, plus a parking lot.

Our good deal just became a great one!

While KCRM Associate Director Steve Kmetz and Chaplain Bill Hunt kept the Walnut Street facility operational, I moved my office to the warehouse on Cherry Street. Demolition began in early February. We gutted the place and began to renovate from the ground up. Progress started out slow, but by early March we were flying.

Volunteers came from everywhere whenever they could. Many gave their evenings after work. Others stayed from first light until dark. Some worked six days a week. Saturdays were intense, Sundays a gift. Help came from many sources.

- Board member Denny Noland handled the drawings and labor for the plumbing.
- A. D. Jacobson, Denny's employer, donated all necessary pipe and fittings, and from their

Roy Campbell *(left)*, assistant project manager, and **Norb Smith**, architect

suppliers, acquired plumbing fixtures for the entire project.

- Jim Hartman supplied a backhoe and an operator to excavate for the underground plumbing.
- Keith Bishop and company handled the concrete work.
- Jim Oberg and John Young laid the bricks and blocks.
- Ken Miller and Burt Schafer did the framing.
- Bill Mullins handled the electrical installation.
- Bill Christie donated the windows.
- Magic Woods Company gave doors, frames, and trim.

As the work progressed, funds began to trickle in, but nowhere near what we needed. Though most of the labor and many materials and supplies were being donated, much would need to be purchased. We eagerly awaited responses from major funders, trusting God to meet the need.

Finally, we heard from Hallmark Cards. "We cannot do what you requested," the representative said.

I had no words.

"You requested $30,000 over a two-year period," the lady continued. "We give only one-time gifts. Also, we've looked into your organization and learned of its history, its roots in the Nazarene Church, and the character of your staff."

I was shocked.

"In light of our policy and our research, we have approved a one-time gift to your organization of $50,000."

Silence followed for many long seconds. Surely I'd misunderstood. Finally I managed, "Could you repeat that, please?" This was unheard of. As I understood it, organizations requesting funds from foundations would often receive, if anything, *less* than requested. Never, more!

She restated the offer. I had heard correctly. Clearly God's resources were being released.

Shortly thereafter the Mabee Foundation in Tulsa, Oklahoma, presented us with a stimulating challenge: If we could raise $757,200 in cash, pledges, and gifts-in-kind toward our newly projected and much more realistic goal of $907,200 by the end of the following February, they would grant the remaining $150,000 needed to complete the project. Talk about incentive.

It seemed as though everyone wanted to help: professionals, union and nonunion workers, handymen, skilled and unskilled laborers, students, staff and board members, the homeless, churches and youth groups, even the children, you name it.

- Grinell Fire Protection supplied all materials for the sprinkler system and arranged for union apprentices to install it.
- The Merten Company designed and installed fire-alarm and paging systems.
- Countertops and windowsills were made and installed by Perry Swofford.
- Brown Industries fabricated the bunk beds and security window screens.

And it just kept happening, all at no cost to the Mission. Volunteers, equipment, and supplies ar-

Some of the 600-plus volunteers

Volunteers raising a chapel wall

rived, at times, almost faster than we knew what to do with them.

April 1 came quickly and with it the sad process of closing down the Walnut Street facility after 28 years. Steve and Chaplain Bill handled the details then joined the rest of us at the Cherry Street property.

Initial progress had been rapid, but by the middle of May, 3½ months into the project, volunteer involvement had diminished, and we were beginning to slow down—fast. This was a much greater undertaking than we'd imagined.

About that time Bob White called. He represented Hallmark Cards and wanted to stop by for a visit and to check on progress. While I was proud to have him come, I was a bit nervous. We had a long way to go and this was a slow day. Several workers hadn't shown up. But then, construction is often like that.

When Bob arrived, we toured the site ending up in the dormitory where Roy Campbell was framing a new wall.

"We'd like to help," Bob announced. That stopped Roy.

They'd already given us nearly twice what we'd asked for. What could they be thinking now?

"Great, what do you have in mind?" Roy asked.

□ □ □ □

**The stunned look on Roy's face,
which must have mirrored mine,
spoke volumes.**

□ □ □ □

Bob said Hallmark liked what they saw and what they'd heard about the Mission. He said the company had a program they thought we might be interested in. Matter-of-factly he explained that, through their Employee Labor Project, Hallmark would send available company employees into the community for periods of time to assist nonprofits, such as KCRM, with building and renovation projects, all at Hallmark's expense. He asked if we were interested.

I'm not sure how long we stood there frozen, but the stunned look on Roy's face, which must have mirrored mine, spoke volumes. Bob's question hardly needed an answer.

After catching our breath, we laid out a plan, outlining exactly what skills would be necessary to complete the renovation. Bob assured us the Hallmarkers could handle it. He said he'd be in touch again soon to set up a schedule.

As Bob drove away Roy asked me to join him in the chapel area. He wept as he explained that, while driving to the Mission that very morning, he'd had a long talk with the Lord. "I told Him everyone's tired," Roy said, "and that this project is bigger than the few volunteers we have left. I asked Him to please send help!"

"I waited patiently for the LORD; He turned to me and heard my cry" (Psalm 40:1).

8

Sheetrock
Evangelism

With the Hallmark team on board, progress accelerated considerably. They ran electrical cable, installed light fixtures, laid floor tile, hung doors, finished woodwork, painted walls, whatever the need, it seemed Hallmark had someone skilled and available to meet it.

Sheetrock, however, was in a class by itself. Work and Witness teams had hung much of it, but we still had 15,000 square feet to go. Denny Noland suggested I contact the Builders Training Center, an organization dedicated to preparing individuals for the building trades. I called and asked if they'd consider sending apprentices to help hang the sheet rock.

Program coordinator, Bill Thomas, toured the site and agreed to assist. For the next few weeks crews of apprentices arrived at the Mission daily. Under the supervision of journeyman instructor Dave Allen, they hung all 15,000 square feet.

Early on we learned that Dave was an atheist. He said he'd tried it all, Christianity included. According to Dave, nothing worked. But, scattered throughout the project were many Christians, including some of the Hallmarkers. Everywhere Dave turned he ran into a believer. Discussions occurred regularly but with no apparent results. When their task was finished, Dave and his crew took off. At least we'd planted a few seeds.

I was surprised to hear his voice a couple weeks later when Dave called asking for Chaplain Bill. He wasn't in at the time.

"Well, I just wanted to tell him thanks," Dave said. "I wanted to thank all you guys for what you did for me while I was there."

"I think we need to thank you, Dave. You guys hung the sheet rock."

"Yeah, but while I was there, I met my Lord and Savior, Jesus Christ!"

□ □ □ □

With slurred speech he managed,
"Either way, Joe, I can't loose."

□ □ □ □

Dave began attending the Southwood Church of the Nazarene where he was instantly accepted, appreciated, and loved. This was a changed man, truly a new creature.

Several weeks later, Dave was diagnosed with cancer. Treatment was ineffective. Surgery was not an option. When I visited with him in the hospital, he was so heavily medicated he was unable to eat and barely able to sit up or even speak.

With slurred speech he managed, "Either way, Joe, I can't lose."

"How's that, Dave?"

"If I live, I'm surrounded by people who love me and care about me. And if I die, I'll be in the arms of my Lord and Savior, Jesus Christ."

Two days later Dave passed away.

So, while KCRM's ministry to the homeless was on hold, the Lord's ministry to the lost continued, and Dave ended up in the Kingdom.

□ □ □ □

We were clearly in the midst of the miracle we'd been praying for, and it continued to unfold.

Ten months after construction began, the doors to our first building opened to the homeless. Then Mayor Emanuel Cleaver of Kansas City officially proclaimed November 14, 1991, as "Kansas City Res-

Mayor Emanuel Cleaver *(left)* presenting proclamation certificate to Carl Lee Aubrey, KCRM board president

Worship service in the new chapel

cue Mission Day." He joined us as we dedicated the building to the Lord's service—just in time for Thanksgiving.

In less than one year we had moved from a deteriorating, century-old building, to a functional state-of-the-art facility, custom-designed to our specifications and valued at more than $1 million. The new complex was nearly three times larger and would eventually accommodate many more people, programs, and services than had been possible at our former location.

The following February 28 at 11:30 P.M. with only 30 minutes to spare, we met the Mabee Foundation challenge and their gift of $150,000 rendered us miraculously debt-free!

For years, long before the River Market redevelopment project forced us to move, we had entertained exciting hopes and dreams. Admittedly, we lacked the means and strategy to achieve them. But now, as a result of what at first appeared to be a fatal blow to the Mission, we'd been launched into a future with a much stronger base of support and a brand new base of operations. Our dreams were within reach.

During the next 13 years, demand for the Mission's assistance would nearly triple. That demand spawned the emergence of several new programs and the renovation of the remaining three buildings in the KCRM complex. Slowly, carefully, we added new staff to accommodate the need, eventually moving from a single employee on that first Super Bowl Sunday to more than 30.

Developing staff and programs took precedence over construction, so after completing building one, which could now accommodate the daily flow of more than 100 homeless clients, it took two years more to complete the renovation of building two, which happened in the same miraculous fashion as the first. This building became living quarters for the participants in our growing Christian Development Program for recovery (CDP), increasing program capacity from 6 to 20 men.

As demand for our services progressively increased the Lord continued to build our team and strengthen our programs. One unique experience illustrates this point.

I received an unexpected long distance call

**Current KCRM staff.
Marilyn and Joe Colaizzi on front row.**

from Illinois one afternoon from a lady I'd never met. She'd been to the Mission once several months earlier while in Kansas City, training as a Nazarene in Volunteer Service (NIVS). She told me that the Lord was calling her to the Kansas City Rescue Mission to volunteer her time. I was skeptical. The Lord hadn't spoken to me about this yet, and at the time we had no staff openings. Although she wanted no salary, she'd need a place to stay, and I wasn't at all sure about having a lady staying in the staff apartment in an all-men's mission. She asked me to pray about it and offered the names of several references. There was no question, according to her references; Marge Chapman was a strong, committed Christian servant. Resistant though I was, the Lord had a plan, and it became progressively clearer that, whether I thought Marge ought to come to the Mission or not, He wanted her here.

When she arrived, we set her up in the apartment and turned her loose. Marge found more to do than I could ever have imagined. She served as janitor, barber, seamstress, dishwasher, kitchen helper, and more. Wherever there was a need, Marge found a way to meet it. Her sweet spirit and servant's attitude soon won the hearts of us all. But it wasn't until our Food Service Manager handed in his resignation that I began to realize how significant Marge's presence was. Without hesitation she stepped in and took the reins to the Mission's food service operation, where she served and ministered for the next four years.

KCRM today

During her stay at the Mission, Marge's friend Irene came to visit. They soon became roommates, and much to my surprise the entire scenario played out again. This time it was Irene who took the reins when Marge retired. With the help of these two ladies and countless others whom the Lord also sent, the Mission team and its programs grew stronger and more stable, paving the way for the next step—renovation of the two remaining buildings in the complex.

Four years after completing building two, we turned our attention to the donated buildings to the north. Building three would become a Transitional Living Center (TLC). It would house a new program designed to reduce recidivism among CDP graduates who need to "test their wings" in a supportive environment, assisting them as they transition from the Mission back into the mainstream of society. Building four would provide space for a maintenance shop, a future job training program, and storage. Once again with donations of cash, building materials, reduced professional fees, the assistance of Hallmark's Employee Labor Project, and a tremendous amount of volunteer labor we accomplished our goal. Today the TLC provides living space for 18 CDP graduates and increases KCRM's recovery program capacity to 38 men. The maintenance shop and storage area are complete. The job-training program is in the works.

With the buildings *transformed* and a strong professional staff in place, much is being accomplished at the Mission these days to *transform* lives.

There is no way to adequately describe all that God is doing and the future we believe He has in store. (For a snapshot of current ministries and future plans, see appendix C.)

9

To the Streets— Again

The Lord has brought the Mission a long way since the early days of "soup, soap, and salvation." The programs are exciting, plans are comprehensive, and the facilities are state-of-the-art. But the real miracles are those of broken lives restored. The following stories are but a few examples of the thousands of lives that have been touched and transformed by Jesus Christ throughout the history of KCRM.

☐ ☐ ☐ ☐

Remember Tim? He's the alcoholic who'd been brutally beaten, left for dead, and consequently suffered amnesia. We worked with him for five years. During those years through the patient efforts of KCRM's staff and Mission-sponsored, Christ-centered Alcoholics Anonymous meetings, Tim eventually found the Lord and forgiveness. He made amends for his reckless past and began a new life. He's been clean and sober for 11 years, the last 7 of which he has served as a youth worker for Missouri's Jackson County family court system, helping troubled youth who are on the same destructive path Tim once walked.

Tim

☐ ☐ ☐ ☐

Yates was driven by a crack cocaine addiction to end it all, but his sister somehow got him away from his "friends" in Illinois and into a Kansas City treatment center. From there he was referred to KCRM's Christian Development Program where he met Jesus and found forgiveness, hope, and the power to overcome his addiction. Next he found a church home, a wife, and a job, which provided insurance to cover unexpected open-heart surgery. I had just entered the intensive care unit to visit Yates when I heard a voice behind calling me, "Hey, Joe." I turned to see Arthur who had once participated in the Mission's recovery program. His was a life shattered by drugs and alcohol. This time, however, he was smiling. As he reached to shake my hand, I noticed the ID tag

Yates

fixed to his uniform, indicating he was a hospital employee. Now I was smiling.

"Joe," he said, "I'm working here in maintenance. I'm back with my family and we're buying a house. I've been free from drugs and alcohol since I left the Mission, and I'm still keeping the main thing the main thing—staying focused on the Lord."

Yates recovered completely from his heart surgery and is doing well. He continues to serve the Lord joyfully as husband, father, and Overnight Shelter Supervisor at the Mission.

▢ ▢ ▢ ▢

Homelessness isn't always a choice. Such was the case with Del. His early years centered around fast cars and gambling. A boxing career led to street fights, broken bones, and countless brushes with the law. But after a four-year stint in the Navy and a short-lived marriage, Del began to settle down. Two solid jobs and 28 years later, depression hit hard and Del's life began to crumble. As the depression became chronic and more severe, he withdrew. Thoughts of suicide began to consume him. He was afraid, empty, alone. Then he lost his apartment, his livelihood, and his self-worth.

Homeless and broken, Del came to the Mission for food and shelter. He was hoping to overcome his

Del

chronic condition but later admitted, "I didn't think I'd ever be lifted out of my depression."

We encouraged him to participate in the Christian Development Program, where he began to establish a personal relationship with the Lord. As the depression subsided, Del found emotional healing, and his hopes were soon restored. When we offered him a job, Del accepted. We were thrilled.

Del's faith grew steadily as he served at the Mission faithfully for 8½ years. Then health problems led to an emergency surgery that, sadly, Del did not survive. The good news? On his way into the operating room, Del confidently announced to the nurse, "I'm all prayed up. Whatever happens, I'm at peace."

☐ ☐ ☐ ☐

A five-year sentence at Central Missouri Correctional Center ended with parole after three years. That brought the total to 26 years served for four-time-loser Terry. At age 48 he'd spent more time in prison than out.

Between jobs and prison stays, he had run drugs, managed massage parlors, robbed supermarkets (for the adrenaline rush), and collected drug money for the outlaw motorcycle club he rode with in California. Violence and crime were a way of life.

☐ ☐ ☐ ☐

**"Get away from me," threatened
Terry, "or I'll break your jaw."**

☐ ☐ ☐ ☐

During a cross-country motorcycle trip, a visit with an old girl friend led to a fight with police and a five year prison sentence in southern Missouri.

With two years yet to serve, Terry was placed on parole. Restricted to Missouri, he headed to Kansas City, wondering why they'd released him, convinced he'd be back in prison again soon. Wasting no time in Kansas City, Terry's first stop netted him a pistol and a bag of heroin. The next three weeks of wild living led to a downtown street corner where a stranger approached him.

"You look like you need some help," the stranger offered.

"Get away from me," threatened Terry, "or I'll break your jaw."

Undaunted, the stranger continued, "Kansas City Rescue Mission has a good recovery program." Then he offered directions. For some unknown reason Terry reluctantly followed those directions, realizing along the way that his "life had become pretty pathetic."

Forrest greeted him at the door with a smile and a "good you came." Terry just listened as Forrest, himself a graduate of the Christian Development Program (CDP), and other program participants encouraged him. Terry spent the weekend listening, waiting, and observing. Others stopped to talk. One was memorizing Bible verses.

"This was interesting," says Terry. "Here were a bunch of rough, coarse guys with not the best language, but they were trying. And in my head the thought kept playing, *I need to do something!*"

On Monday, Terry became the newest participant in the CDP and began to walk away from his troubled past.

The next six months were not easy for Terry. "Coming to Christ was a process," he says, "not just an overnight thing. Lots of times I was ready to leave, but something would take place, and I'd say, 'OK, let's try another day.' My mind cleared slowly, and more understanding came. Life just started to make more sense."

After graduating from the program Terry moved to the Mission's Transitional Living Center and enrolled in a community college where he spent the next two years earning A's and B's. His next step is a degree in social work. "Or, maybe Bible college for Christian counseling," he says. "I'm not sure yet, something to help others. It's on my heart to take what I've lived through and use it to help others who don't feel there's any way out. I believe the Lord has called me to this."

In contrast to his old life in which every day was based on outlaw behavior—sex, drugs, drinking, and crime—Terry says, "My life now is based around pleasing God and making amends for the wrongs I've done by doing what God wants."

Terry still rides his bike, but he's traded involvement with the outlaw motorcycle club for a membership in the Christian Motorcycle Association (CMA). School, CMA involvement, and a job keep Terry busy. Recently and prayerfully he and his sweetheart, Bev, were married. With the Lord's help

Terry and Bev

he's patching up fractured relationships with his daughter and his sister.

"Since I have Jesus in my heart," Terry says, "I'm happy and at peace. Looking back, I can see God at work through it all, and the work is still going on continually."

Epilogue

The story continues,
Terry's story, my story, your story,
His story.
It is not yet complete.

"Being confident of this,
that he who began a good work in you
will carry it on to completion
until the day of Christ Jesus"
(Philippians 1:6).

Appendix

A. Locations of the Kansas City Rescue Mission all in Kansas City, Missouri:

1. 916 East 12 St. (1950)
2. 918 East 12 St. (1951)
3. 702 East 12 St. (1953)
4. 710 East 12 St. (1955)
5. 523 Walnut St. (1962)
6. 1520 Cherry St. (1991)

B. Leaders of Kansas City Rescue Mission since its founding:

1. James and Carol Kratz (1950)
2. D. H. Tracy (1951)
3. Bert and Thelma Hotchkiss (1954)
4. Eugene Lain (1960)
5. Bert Hotchkiss (1962)
6. Harold L. Browning (1966)
7. Adam Hoffpauir (1970)
8. Wes Peterson (1978)
9. David Blackburn (1981)
10. Tim Kilby and Jim and Mary Spaid (1983)
11. Joe and Marilyn Colaizzi (1985)

C. KCRM Ministries (2004)

1. Chaplaincy:

   - Provides nightly English and Spanish language chapel services, discipleship classes, and pastoral counseling orchestrated by three chaplains, two of whom are bilingual.

   - Presents weekly Christian videos in both Spanish and English; offers monthly board game activities.

   - Assists with case management among Spanish-speaking clients.

   - Realizes average annual responses to the gospel numbering 895 and an average of 379 who accept Christ as Lord and Savior.

2. Case Management:

   - Assists homeless clients with acquisition of proper identification, eye glasses, housing (annual average 89), and employment (annual average 65).

   - Manages "Steps-Toward-Success," a program that holds employed clients accountable to reach their goals for savings and housing.

   - Provides more than 1,400 referrals to area social service agencies annually.

   - Collaborates with other homeless serving agencies, strengthening KCRM's relationships within the community.

3. Christian Development Program:

   - Facilitates the process of recovery and Christian growth among an average of 65 men annually.

- Offers basic and advanced computer training and computer-based GED classes.
- Oversees KCRM's Transitional Living Center.
- Sends qualified graduates to the Missouri Vocational Rehabilitation to assist with education, preemployment preparation, and employment opportunities.

4. Food Service Ministry:

- Serves an average of 65,270 balanced, nutritious meals annually.
- Trains and maintains a professional staff of health department-certified food service workers.
- Nurtures and trains Christian Development Program participants assigned to food service duty.
- Regularly serves as a resource to other community providers of food service to the poor.

5. Shelter:

- Assists an average of 1,774 homeless people annually.
- Provides safe comfortable shelter for an average of 85 men per night.
- Manages a neighborhood clean-up campaign among the homeless.
- Coordinates a recuperation program for the homeless with area hospitals.

6. Development:

- Handles donor relations and public awareness of KCRM.

- Manages KCRM's donor base, increasing it from 1,500 to 12,000 in 10 years.
- Communicates with and coordinates activities for more than 2,200 volunteers annually.
- Developed and maintains KCRM's web site: <www.kcrm.org>.

7. Volunteer and cooperative ministries:

- Provide Christ-centered Alcoholics Anonymous and Alcoholics Victorious meetings weekly.
- Organize and issue clothing to homeless clients weekly.
- Assist clients with income tax preparation and hair cuts.
- Conduct an average 1,400 health clinic appointments annually with assistance from MidAmerica Nazarene University, local nurses, Swope Health Services, and area hospitals.
- Offer English as a second language classes to Spanish-speaking clients.
- Provide Christian legal aid to the homeless in cooperation with the Christian Legal Society.
- Offers the Phineas Bresee Urban Mission Scholarship through Nazarene Theological Seminary to qualified seminary students.

The future looks more exciting still. Our vision is this: "People served by KCRM are able to live successfully on their own in balanced interdependent lives with Christ." To accomplish this, our mission is to offer "freedom and hope to the poor and homeless, empowering them to reach their full potential."

Sample plans include:
- job readiness and life skills training
- addressing the community's need for permanent affordable housing
- expanded health services
- programs and services for women, children, and families
- establishing an endowment
- launching an income-generating business
- developing and strengthening KCRM's partnerships within the community